Variegated FLORAL BORDERS

40 CROSS-STITCH PATTERNS BY LINDA GILLUM

Working with variegated floss is fun and creates an automatic depth of color and complexity which will bring amazing results. The method used for stitching these borders with variegated threads was completely random. The floss was not cut in a particular place and the thread was not manipulated for color placement. Each cross stitch was completed individually. You may want to experiment with other methods of stitching with variegated flosses. Stitching from light to dark shades, in random swirls of color, with purposeful placement of colors, or by adding a solid color to a strand of variegated floss are a few options.

Enjoy!

Table of Contents

Autumn Vines....................8

Blooming Fun 9

Bluebirds in My Garden.........................10

Blush Roses.....................11

Bright Banding....................12

Buzzing Bouquets......................13

Carnation Parade 14

Checkered Path.....................15

Climbing Roses......................16

Columbine Cheer 17

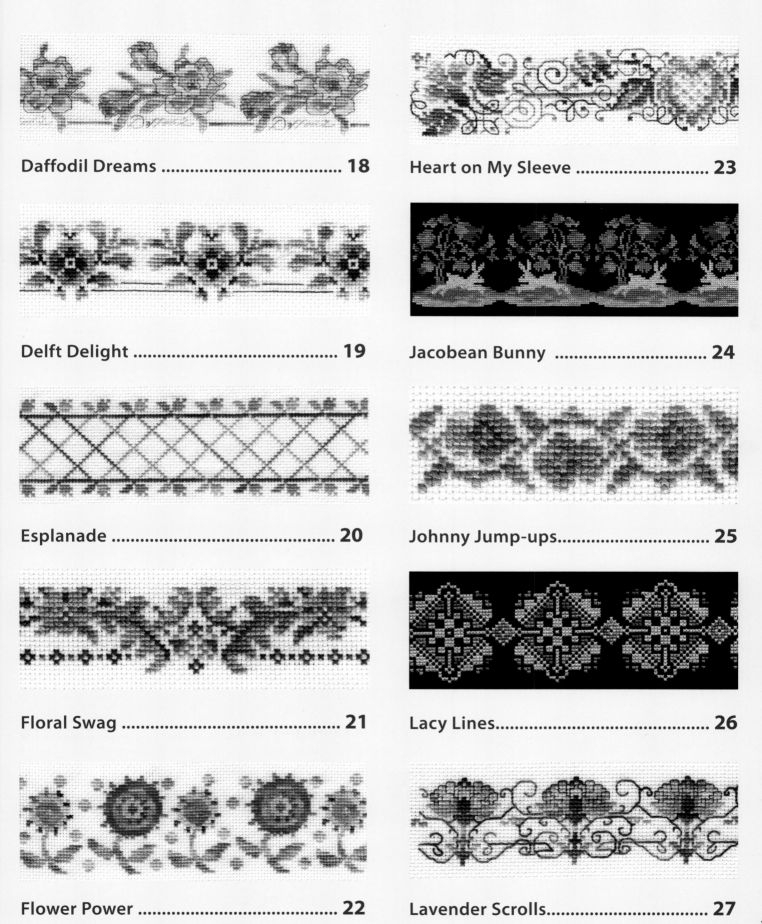

Daffodil Dreams 18

Heart on My Sleeve 23

Delft Delight 19

Jacobean Bunny 24

Esplanade 20

Johnny Jump-ups.......................... 25

Floral Swag 21

Lacy Lines.......................... 26

Flower Power 22

Lavender Scrolls.......................... 27

March of the Marigolds..........................28

Meandering Buds.................................29

Peachy Border 30

Petite Posies.....................................31

Pretty Pomegranates.............................32

Prim and Proper 33

Purple Silhouette 34

Raspberry Vines 35

Rose Beauties 36

Snow Flurries.....................................37

Star Shine 38

Thistle Time 43

Sweet Cherries 39

Topsy Turvy Florals 44

Spring Garden Ribbon 40

Tulip Trail 45

Sunny Swirls............................41

Green Luck 46

Time for Tulips 42

Zinnia Zing............................47

General Instructions ...

Stitching Tips

Preparing Fabric
Cut fabric desired size, allowing at least a 3" margin around the design. Overcast raw edges. It is better to waste a little fabric than to come up short after hours of stitching!

Working with Floss
To ensure smoother stitches, separate strands and realign them before threading needle. Keep stitching tension consistent. Begin and end floss by running under several stitches on back; never tie knots.

Stitch Using Two Different DMC Products
1. DMC Six Strand Embroidery Floss – Article 117. This floss has 454 solid and 18 variegated colors.
2. DMC Six Strand Color Variation Embroidery Floss – Article 417. This floss has 36 variegated colors. An asterisk (*) after color number in key indicates Color Variation.

Where to Start
The horizontal and vertical centers of each charted design are shown by arrows. You may start at any point on the charted design, but be sure the design will be centered on the fabric. Locate the center of fabric by folding in half, top to bottom and again left to right. On the charted design, count the number of squares (stitches) from the center of the chart to where you wish to start. Then from the fabric's center, find your starting point by counting out the same number of fabric threads (stitches).

Working With Charts

How To Read Charts: Each design is shown in chart form. Each symbol square on the charts represents one Cross Stitch. Colored dots represent French Knots. The straight lines on the charts indicate Backstitch. Complete the Cross Stitches before working Backstitches, and French Knots. Bring the needle up at 1 and all odd numbers and down at 2 and all even numbers.

Symbol Key: The symbol key indicates the color of floss to use for each stitch on the chart. Symbol key columns should be read vertically and horizontally to determine type of stitch and floss color. The following headings are given:

DMC — DMC color number

X — Cross Stitch

1/4 — Quarter Cross Stitch

BS — Backstitch

FK — French Knot

Str — Strands

Counted Cross Stitch (X): Work one Cross Stitch to correspond to each symbol square on the chart. For horizontal rows, work stitches in two journeys (Fig. 1). For variegated thread, complete each stitch as shown (Fig. 2).

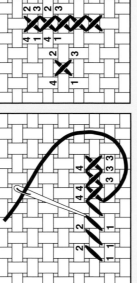

Fig. 1

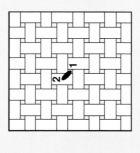

Fig. 2

Quarter Stitch (1/4): Quarter Stitches are denoted by triangular symbols on the chart and on the symbol key. Come up at 1, then split fabric thread to go down at 2 (Fig. 4).

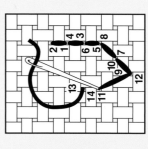

Fig. 4

French Knot (FK): Bring needle up at 1. Wrap floss once around needle and insert needle at 2, holding end of floss with non-stitching fingers (Fig. 3). Tighten knot, then pull needle through fabric, holding floss until it must be released. Stitch with one strand of floss unless otherwise instructed. For larger knot, use more strands; wrap only once.

Fig. 3

Backstitch (BS): For outline detail, Backstitch (shown on chart and on symbol key by colored straight lines) should be worked after the design has been completed (Fig. 5). Stitch with one strand of floss unless otherwise instructed. When the chart shows a Backstitch crossing a symbol square, a Cross Stitch (Fig. 1 or 2) should be worked first, then the Backstitch should be worked on top of the Cross Stitch.

Fig. 5

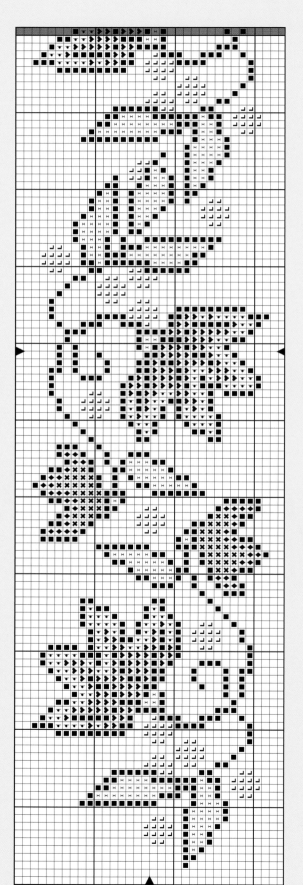

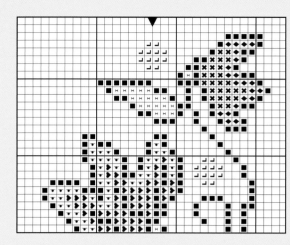

DMC Variegated	X	Str	Color	DMC Variegated	X	Str	Color
4040*	◆	3	Color variations	4190*	▼	3	Color variations
4045*	■	3	Color variations	4200*	▶	3	Color variations
4060*	⊢	3	Color variations	4215*	✖	3	Color variations
4126*	L	3	Color variations				

Autumn Vines 134w x 30h

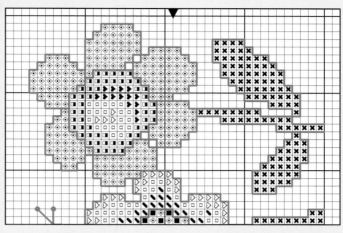

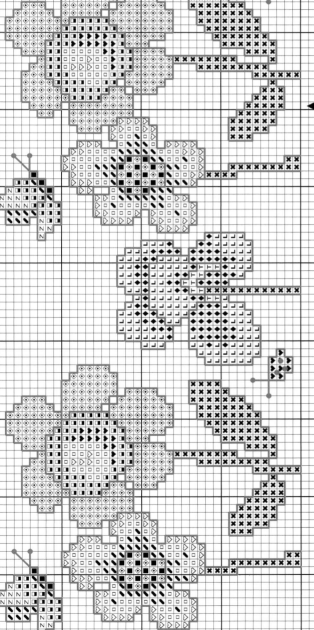

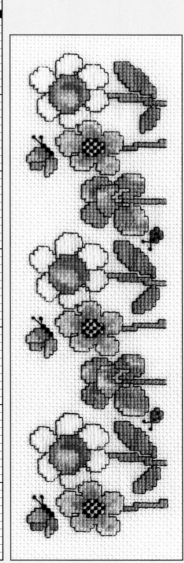

DMC Variegated	X	BS	FK	Str	Color	DMC Variegated	X	Str	Color
310	■			3	Black	4170	▷	3	Color variations
310		╱	●	1	Black	4180*	□	3	Color variations
White	◇			3	White	4190*	◣	3	Color variations
4050*	✖			3	Color variations	4200*	▶	3	Color variations
4077*	T			3	Color variations	4215*	◆	3	Color variations
4100*	N			3	Color variations	4220*	∟	3	Color variations
4124*	◨			3	Color variations				

Blooming Fun 137w x 38h

9

DMC Variegated	X	Str	Color		DMC Variegated	X	Str	Color
4045*	✕	3	Color variations		4190*	▶	3	Color variations
4050*	⌐	3	Color variations		4215*	H	3	Color variations
4124*	◥	3	Color variations		4230*	⌐	3	Color variations

Bluebirds in My Garden 138w x 35h

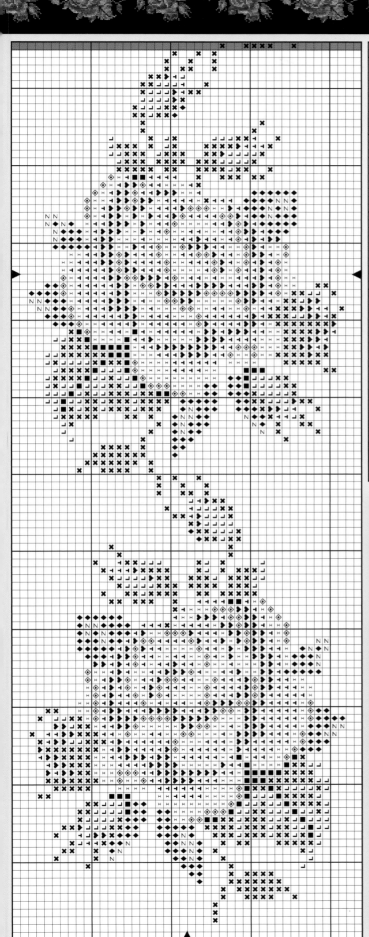

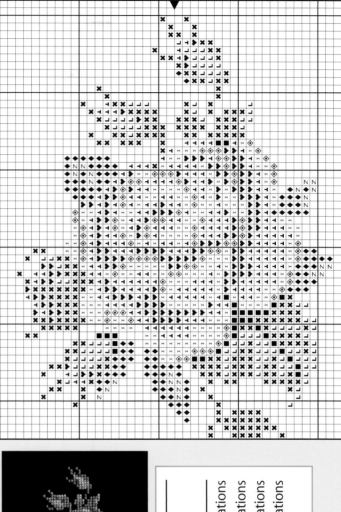

DMC			
Variegated X Str Color			
White	◇	3	White
	◆	3	Color variations
4030*	☒	3	Color variations
4040*	■	3	Color variations
4045*	✖	3	Color variations
4050*		3	Color variations

DMC			
Variegated X Str Color			
4060*	⌐	3	Color variations
4180*	⊢	3	Color variations
4190*	⊣	3	Color variations
4200*	▶	3	Color variations

Blush Roses 168w x 40h

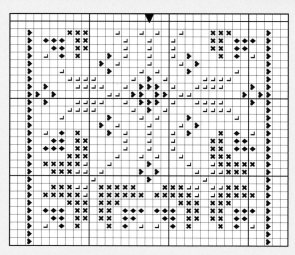

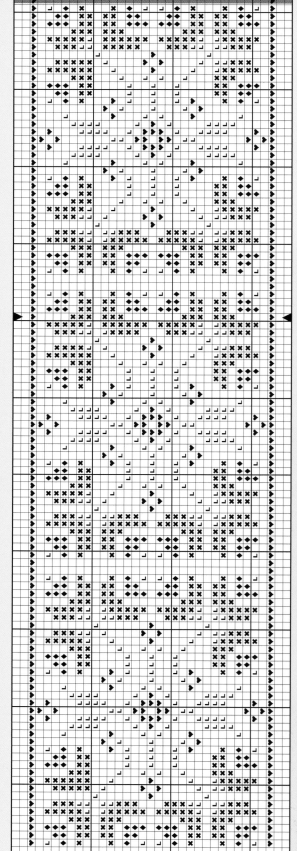

Bright Banding 137w x 31h

DMC Variegated	X		Str	Color
4025*	✖		3	Color variations
4040*	◆		3	Color variations
4050*	L		3	Color variations
4100*	▶		3	Color variations

12

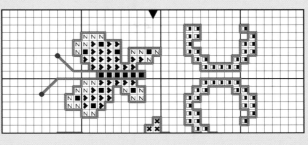

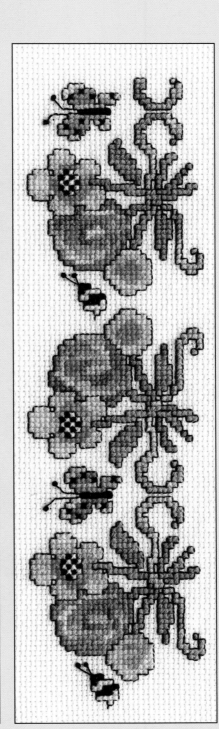

DMC Variegated	X	BS	FK	Str	Color
White	◈			3	White
310	■			3	Black
310		◹	●	1	Black
4030*	◆			3	Color variations
4040*	□			3	Color variations
4050*	✖			3	Color variations

DMC Variegated	X	BS	FK	Str	Color
4077*	◰			3	Color variations
4100*	◥			3	Color variations
4180*	◩			3	Color variations
4190*	▶			3	Color variations
4220*	◱			3	Color variations

Buzzing Bouquets 125w x 34h

13

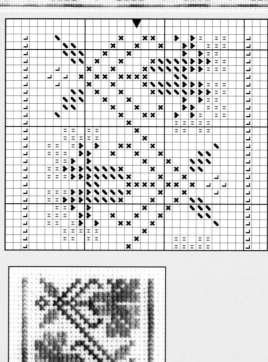

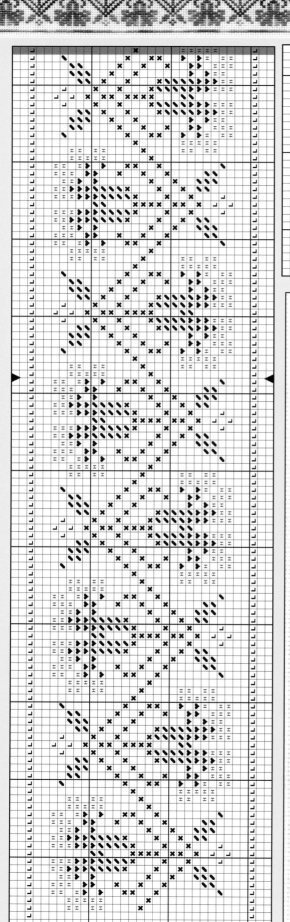

14

DMC Variegated	X	Str	Color
4045*	✖	3	Color variations
4050*	◣	3	Color variations
4190*	H	3	Color variations

DMC Variegated	X	Str	Color
4200*	▶	3	Color variations
4235*	L	3	Color variations

Carnation Parade 140w x 29h

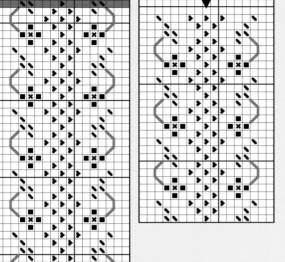

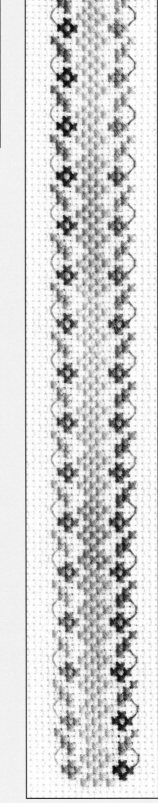

DMC Variegated	X	BS	Str	Color
48	▶		3	Variegated baby pink
52	■		3	Variegated violet
90	✖		3	Variegated yellow

DMC Variegated	X	BS	Str	Color
94		◣	3	Variegated khaki green
94		◹	1	Variegated khaki green

Checkered Path 137w x 13h

15

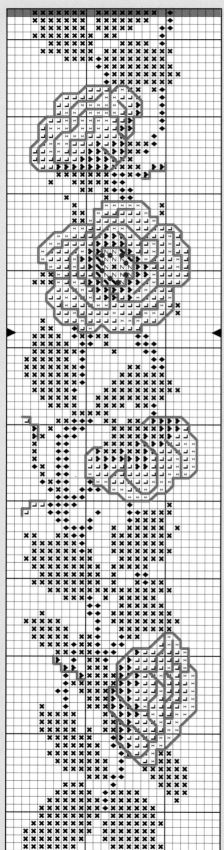

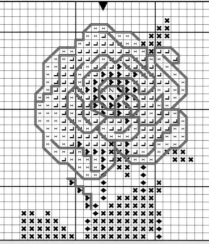

DMC Variegated	X	BS	FK	Str	Color
3799	⬚			3	Pewter Gray-VY DK
4050*	✖			3	Color variations
4124*	◥			3	Color variations
4128*	N			3	Color variations
4140*	◆			3	Color variations

DMC Variegated	X	BS	FK	Str	Color
4140*			●	1	
4170*	H			3	Color variations
4190*	L			3	Color variations
4200*	▶			3	Color variations

Climbing Roses 140w x 23h

16

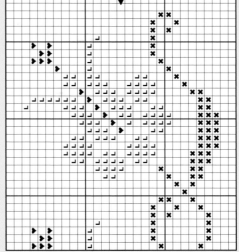

DMC Variegated	X	Str	Color		
4050*	✖	3	Color variations		
4075*	⌐	3	Color variations		
4126*	▶	3	Color variations		

Columbine Cheer 142w x 25h

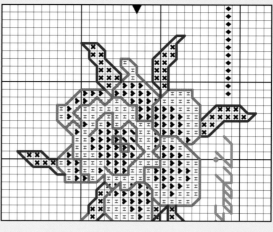

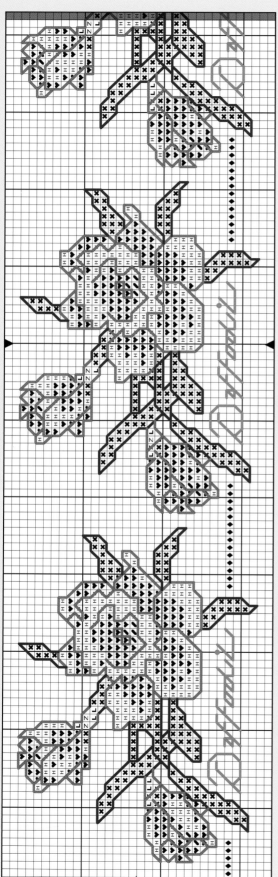

DMC Variegated	X	BS	FK	Str	Color
841	L			3	Beige brown-LT
842	Z			3	Beige brown-VY LT
3826	◣			3	Golden brown
3826			◿	3	Golden brown
4070*	✖			3	Color variations

DMC Variegated	X	BS	FK	Str	Color
4070*		◹		1	Color variations
4077*	H			3	Color variations
4120*	▶			3	Color variations
4230*	◆			3	Color variations
4240*		◿	●	1	Color variations

Daffodil Dreams 140w × 30h

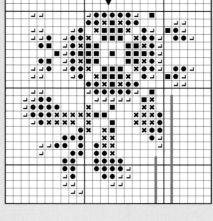

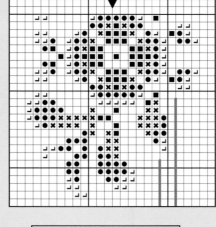

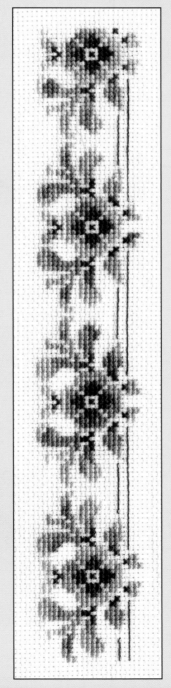

DMC Variegated	X	BS	Str	Color
4010*	L		3	Color variations
4215*	X		3	Color variations
4230*	●		3	Color variations

DMC Variegated	X	BS	Str	Color
4240*	■		3	Color variations
4240*		◿	1	

Delft Delight 138w x 22h

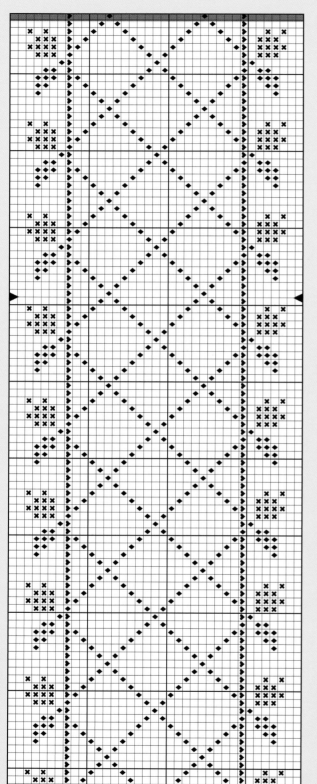

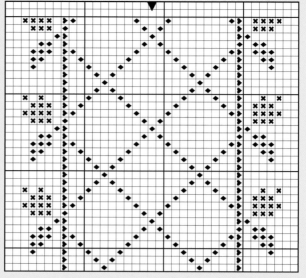

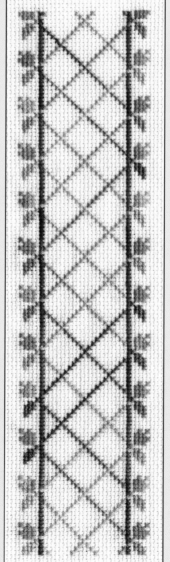

DMC Variegated	X	Str	Color
94	◆ ▶	3	Variegated khaki green
4130*	▶	3	Color variations
4190*	✖	3	Color variations

Esplanade 138w x 33h

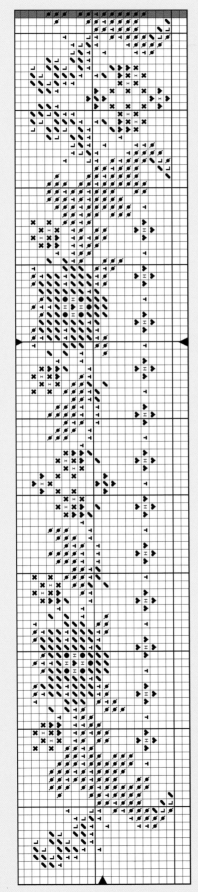

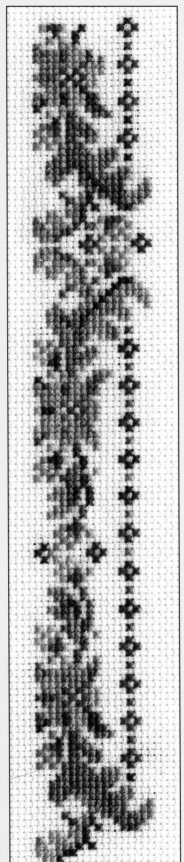

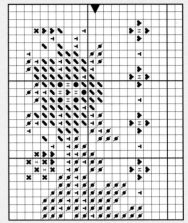

DMC Variegated	X	Str	Color			DMC Variegated	X	Str	Color
4045*	⊣	3	Color variations			4130*	●	3	Color variations
4065*	◣	3	Color variations			4170*	⊦	3	Color variations
4070*	L	3	Color variations			4190*	✖	3	Color variations
4075*	⊦	3	Color variations			4210*	▶	3	Color variations
4126*	◥	3	Color variations						

Floral Swag 136w x 18h

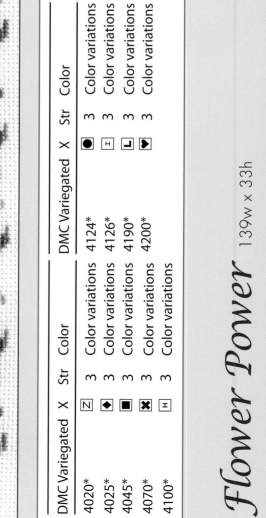

DMC Variegated	X	Str	Color
4020*	N	3	Color variations
4025*	◆	3	Color variations
4045*	■	3	Color variations
4070*	✖	3	Color variations
4100*	H	3	Color variations

DMC Variegated	X	Str	Color
4124*	●	3	Color variations
4126*	H	3	Color variations
4190*	L	3	Color variations
4200*	▶	3	Color variations

Flower Power 139w x 33h

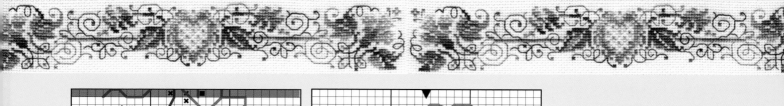

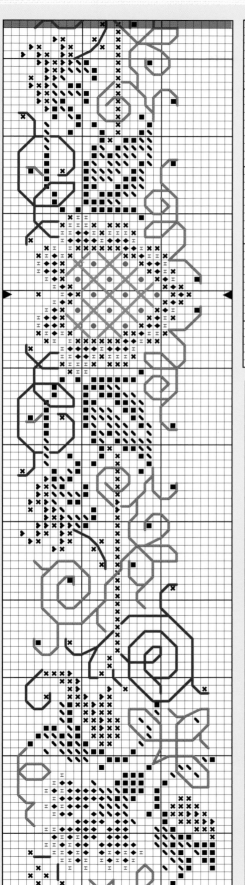

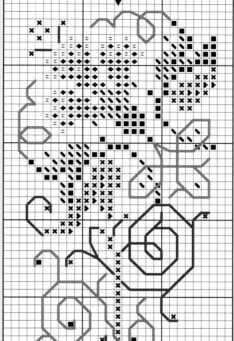

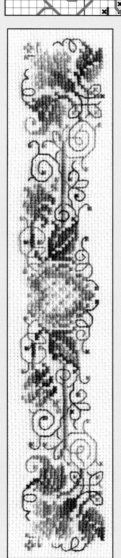

DMC Variegated	X	BS	FK	Str	Color	DMC Variegated	X	BS	FK	Str	Color
4045*	■			3	Color variations	4160*	H			3	Color variations
4045*		◪		2	Color variations	4160*		◪		2	Color variations
4065*	✖			3	Color variations	4215*	✖			3	Color variations
4065*			◉	1	Color variations	4215*		◪		2	Color variations
4120*	◆			3	Color variations	4220*	▶			3	Color variations

Heart on My Sleeve 155w x 25h

23

DMC Variegated	X	BS	Str	Color
White	◈		3	White
4045*	■		3	Color variations
4045*		◪	1	Color variations
4050*	L		3	Color variations
4070*	✖		3	Color variations

DMC Variegated	X	BS	Str	Color
4080*	H		3	Color variations
4128*	⌐		3	Color variations
4160*	N		3	Color variations
4200*	▶		3	Color variations
4215*	◆		3	Color variations

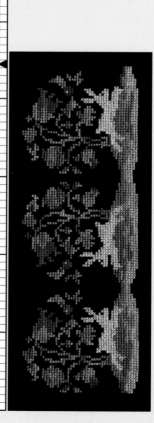

Jacobean Bunny 130w x 46h

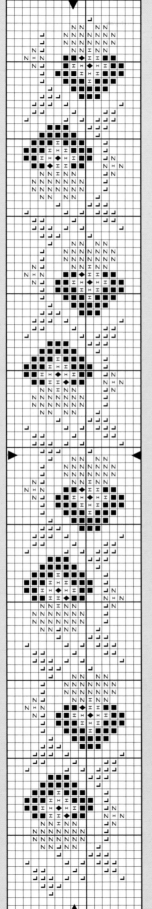

Johnny Jump-ups 114w × 13h

DMC Variegated	X	Str	Color		DMC Variegated		Str	Color
740	◆	3	Tangerine		4050*	∟	3	Color variations
742	⊞	3	Tangerine-LT		4215*	■	3	Color variations
4045*	⊟	3	Color variations		4220*	Z	3	Color variations

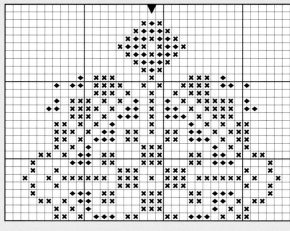

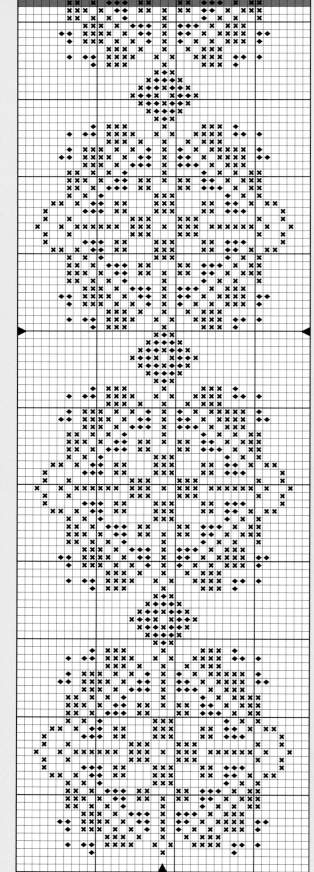

DMC Variegated	X	Str	Color
4145*	◆	3	Color variations
4150*	✖	3	Color variations

Lacy Lines 136w × 33h

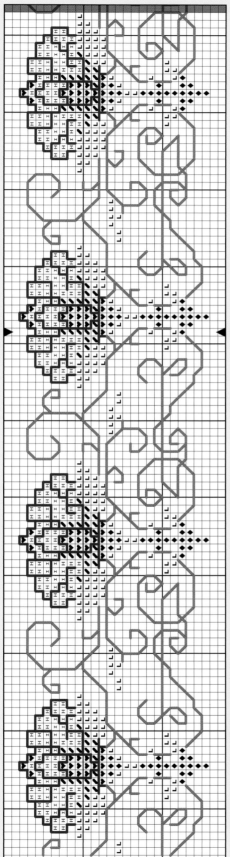

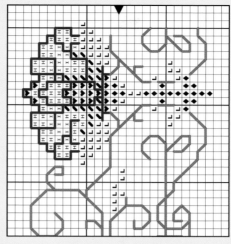

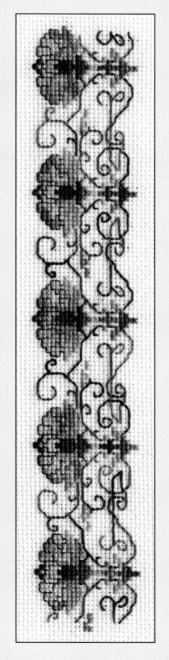

DMC Variegated	X	BS	Str	Color	DMC Variegated	X	BS	Str	Color
4010*	H		3	Color variations	4240*	◆		3	Color variations
4045*	◆		3	Color variations	4240*		◸	1	Color variations
4070*		◸	1	Color variations	4230*	H		3	Color variations
4215*	◥		3	Color variations					

Lavender Scrolls 139w x 24h

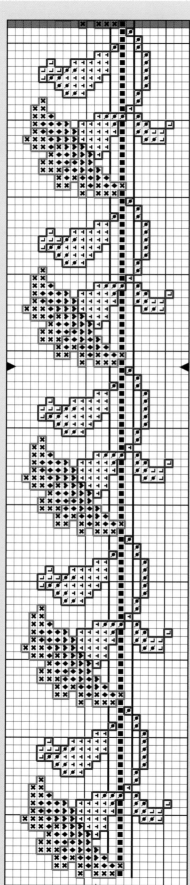

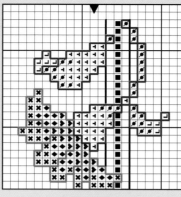

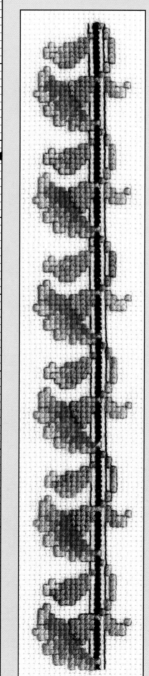

DMC Variegated	X	BS	Str	Color	DMC Variegated	X	BS	Str	Color
310	■		3	Black	4100*	✖		3	Color variations
310		◪	1		4124*	◆		3	Color variations
4045*		◪	1	Color variations	4200*	▶		3	Color variations
4050*	⊞		3	Color variations	4200*		◲	1	
4070*	◪		3	Color variations	4060*	∟		3	Color variations

March of the Marigolds 132w x 19h

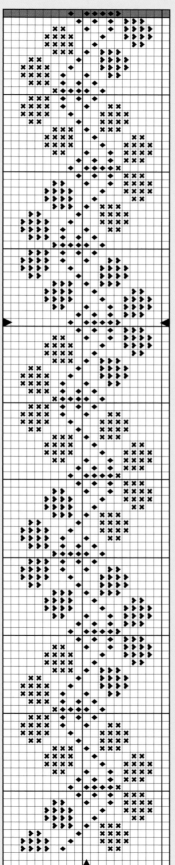

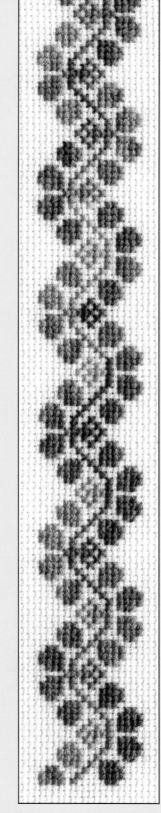

DMC Variegated	X	Str	Color
94	◆	3	Variegated khaki green
4030*	✖	3	Color variations
4215*	▶	3	Color variations

Meandering Buds 137w x 17h

29

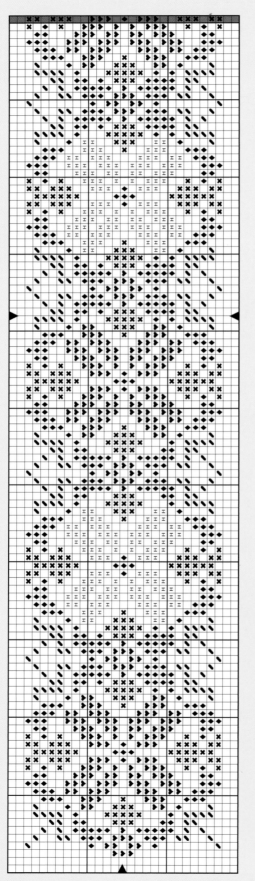

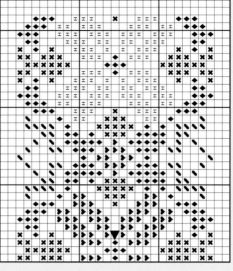

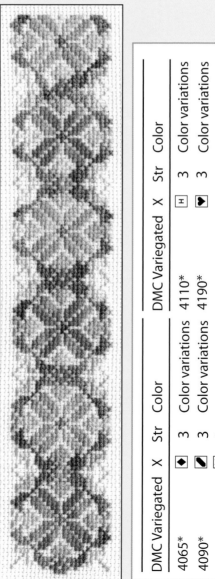

DMC Variegated	X	Str	Color	
4065*	◆	3	Color variations	
4090*	◣	3	Color variations	
4100*	✖	3	Color variations	

DMC Variegated	X	Str	Color	
4110*	H	3	Color variations	
4190*	▶	3	Color variations	

Peachy Border 140w x 25h

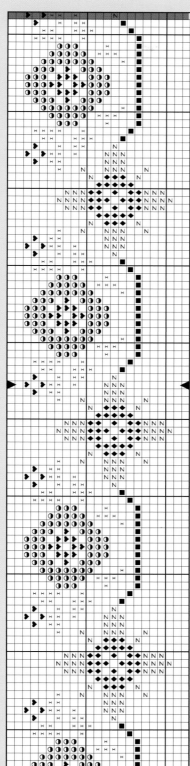

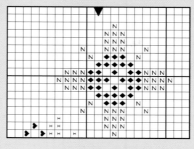

DMC Variegated	X	Str	Color			DMC Variegated	X	Str	Color
4070*	H	3	Color variations			4190*	◆	3	Color variations
4120*	◑	3	Color variations			4200*	▶	3	Color variations
4180*	Z	3	Color variations			4215*	■	3	Color variations

Petite Posies 125w x 19h

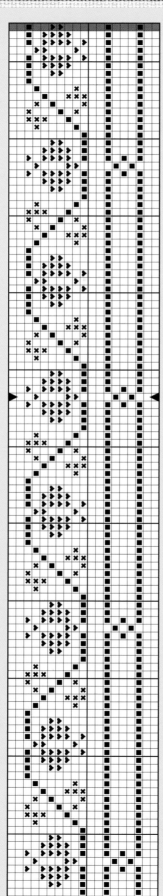

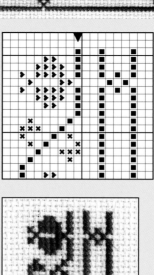

Pretty Pomegranates 129w x 15h

DMC Variegated	X	Str	Color
103	■	3	Variegated royal blue
4045*	✖	3	Color variations
4210*	▶	3	Color variations

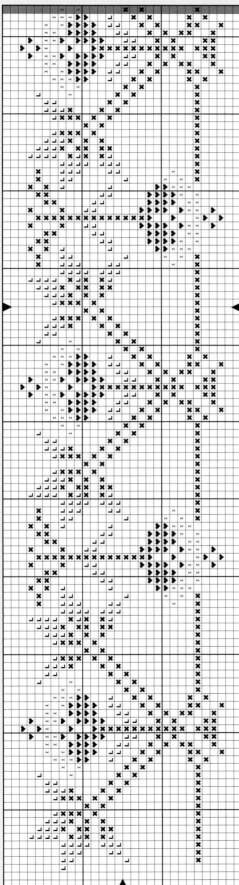

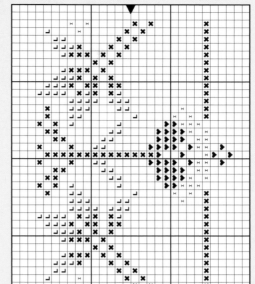

Prim and Proper 146w x 26h

DMC Variegated	X	Str	Color		
4045*	✖		3	Color variations	
4050*	⌐		3	Color variations	
4190*	н		3	Color variations	
4200*	▶		3	Color variations	

33

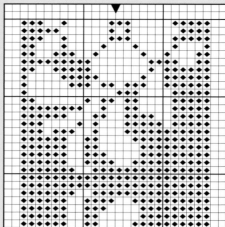

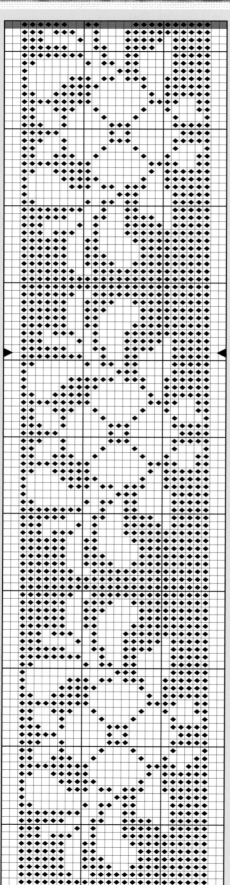

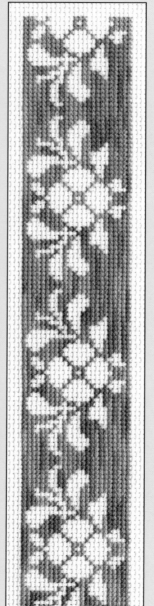

DMC Variegated	X	Str	Color
			Color variations
4215*	◆	3	

Purple Silhouette 138w x 24h

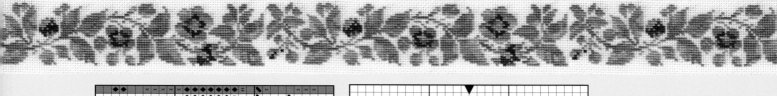

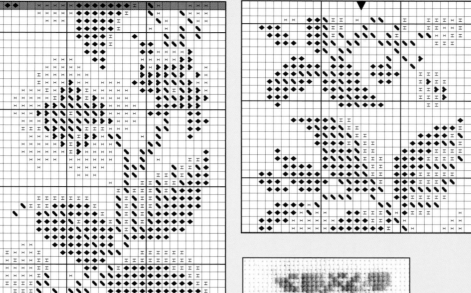

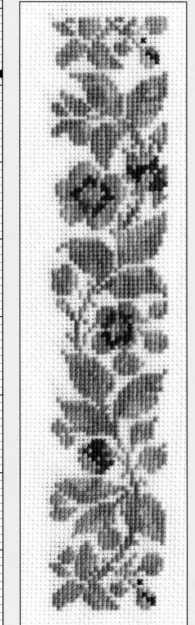

DMC Variegated	X	Str	Color	DMC Variegated	X	Str	Color
4050*	◆	3	Color variations	4190*	⊞	3	Color variations
4070*	⊞	3	Color variations	4210*	◥	3	Color variations
4128*	◣	3	Color variations				

Raspberry Vines 139w x 26h

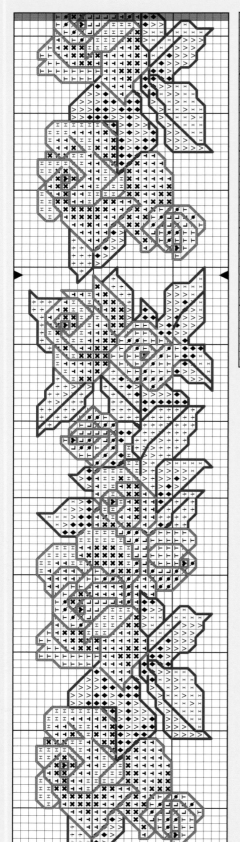

Rose Beauties 154w x 23h

DMC Variegated	X	BS	Str	Color
4040*	⊟		3	Color variations
4045*	◆		3	Color variations
4045*		◹	1	Color variations
4050*	∨		3	Color variations
4070*	✚		3	Color variations
4100*	⊣		3	Color variations
4120*	✖		3	Color variations

DMC Variegated	X	BS	Str	Color
4060*	⊟		3	Color variations
4170*	⊤		3	Color variations
4180*	◹		3	Color variations
4190*	∟		3	Color variations
4200*	▶		3	Color variations
4200*		◹	3	Color variations
4200*			1	Color variations

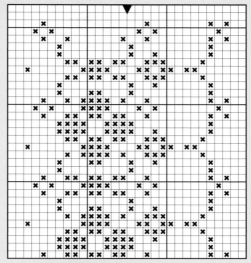

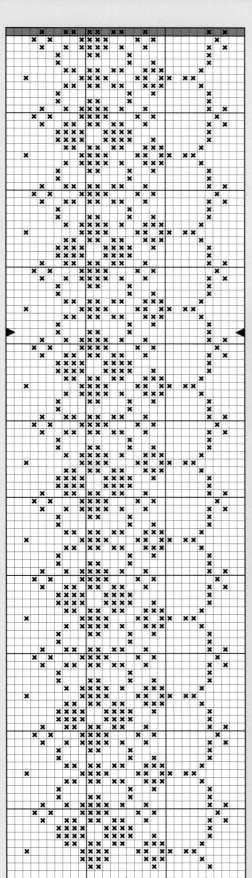

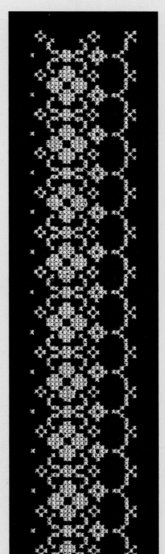

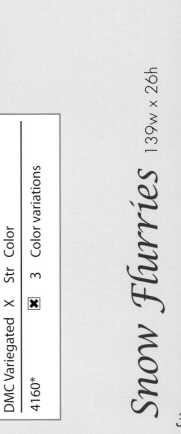

Snow Flurries 139w x 26h

DMC Variegated	X	Str	Color
4160*	⊠	3	Color variations

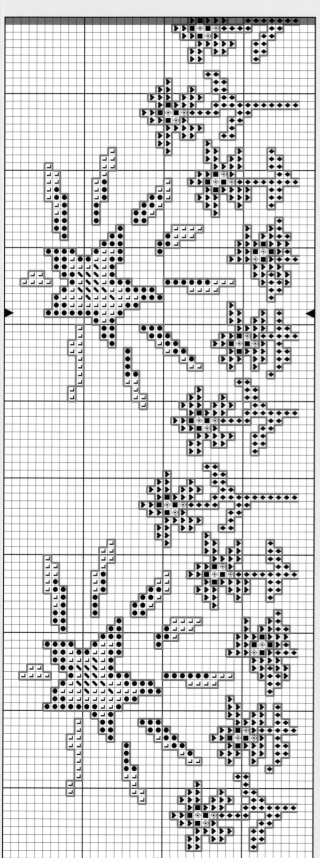

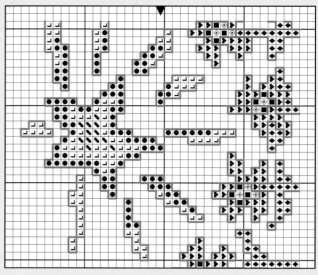

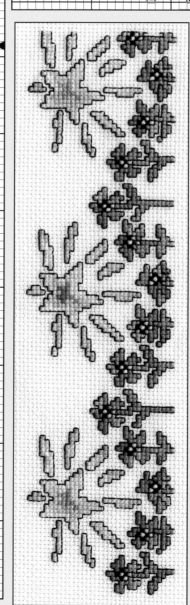

DMC Variegated	X	BS	Str	Color		DMC Variegated	X	BS	Str	Color
White	⊠		3	White		4077*	●		3	Color variations
310	■		3	Black		4100*	⌐		3	Color variations
310		⟋	1			4124*	◩		3	Color variations
4050*	◆		3	Color variations		4190*	▶		3	Color variations

Star Shine 139w x 35h

38

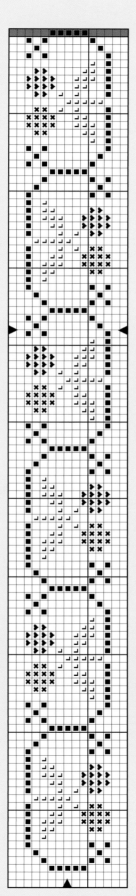

DMC Variegated	X	Str	Color
4070*	L	3	Color variations
4110*	✗	3	Color variations
4126*	■	3	Color variations
4190*	▶	3	Color variations

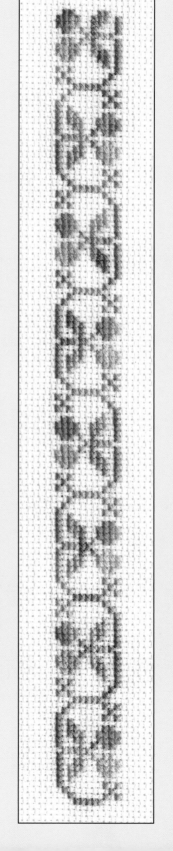

Sweet Cherries 140w x 11h

39

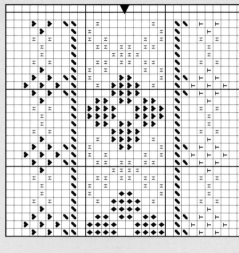

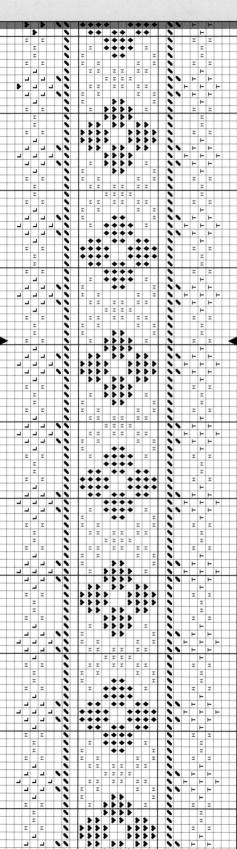

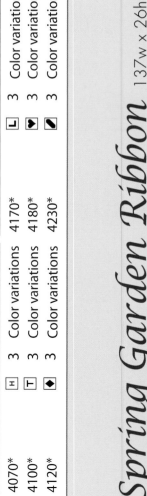

Spring Garden Ribbon 137w x 26h

DMC Variegated	X	Str	Color		DMC Variegated	X	Str	Color
4070*	H	3	Color variations		4170*	L	3	Color variations
4100*	T	3	Color variations		4180*	▶	3	Color variations
4120*	◆	3	Color variations		4230*	◥	3	Color variations

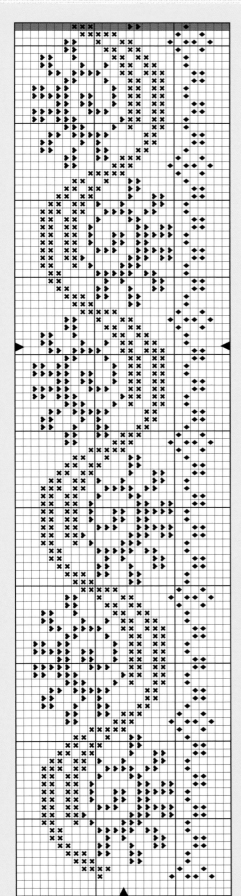

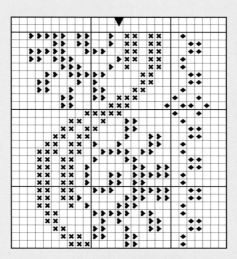

DMC Variegated	X	Str	Color
52	◆	3	Variegated violet
4070*	✖	3	Color variations
4120*	▶	3	Color variations

Sunny Swirls 138w x 23h

41

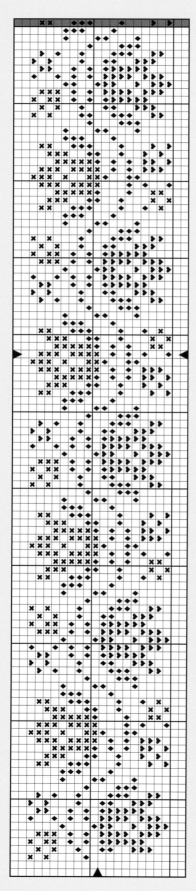

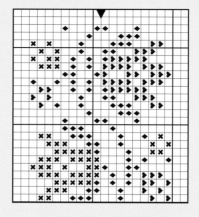

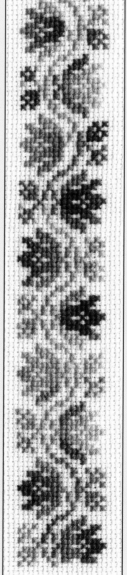

DMC Variegated	X	Str	Color
94	◆	3	Variegated khaki green
99	▶	3	Variegated mauve
111	✖	3	Variegated mustard

Time for Tulips 131w × 18h

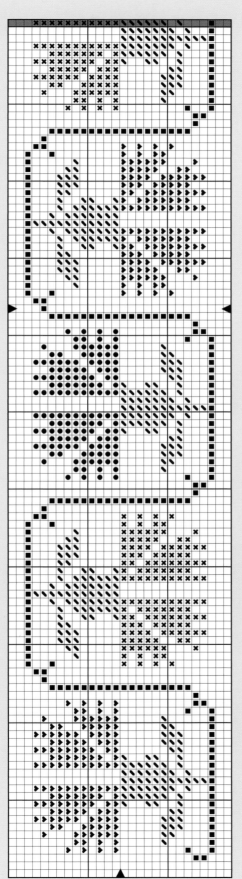

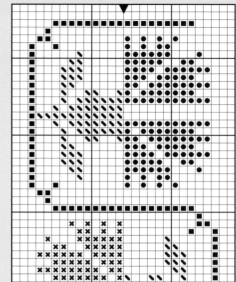

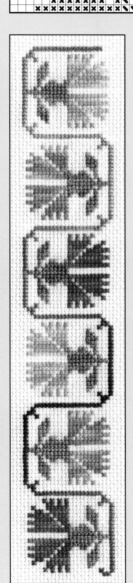

DMC Variegated	X	Str	Color	DMC Variegated	X	Str	Color
111	■	3	Variegated mustard	4190*	✖	3	Color variations
4050*	◥	3	Color variations	4200*	▶	3	Color variations
4180*	●	3	Color variations				

Thistle Time 143w x 24h

43

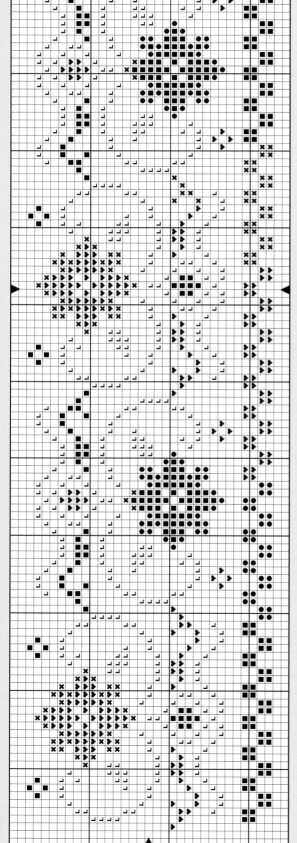

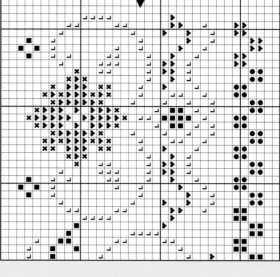

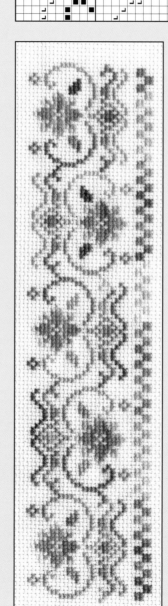

DMC Variegated	X	Str	Color
94	L	3	Variegated khaki green
4100*	●	3	Color variations
4124*	■	3	Color variations

DMC Variegated	X	Str	Color
4170*	✖	3	Color variations
4190*	▶	3	Color variations

Topsy Turvy Florals 140w x 31h

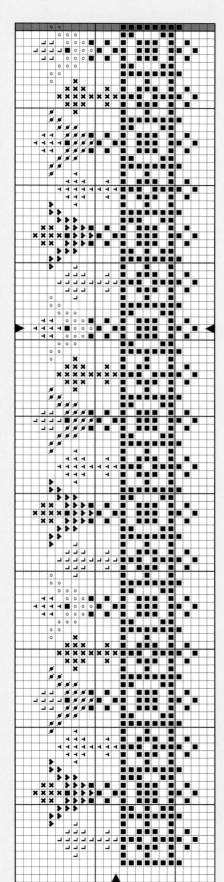

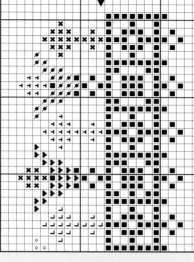

DMC Variegated	X	Str	Color
125	■	3	Variegated seafoam green
4010*	✖	3	Color variations
4020*	○	3	Color variations
4060*	┙	3	Color variations

DMC Variegated	X	Str	Color
4077*	┕	3	Color variations
4120*	▶	3	Color variations
4180*	◢	3	Color variations

Tulip Trail 139w x 21h

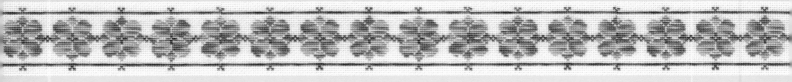

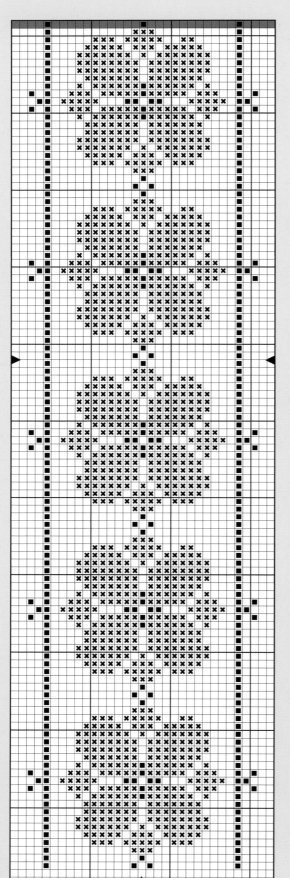

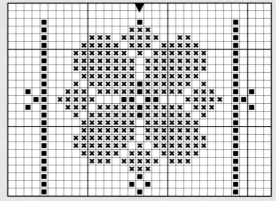

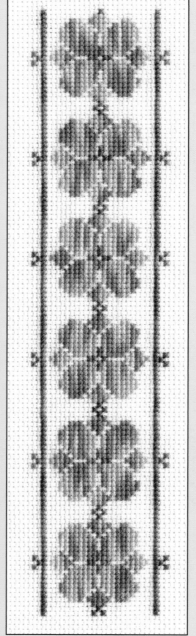

Green Luck 132w x 29h

DMC Variegated	X	Str	Color	
4030*	■	3	Color variations	
4040*	✕	3	Color variations	

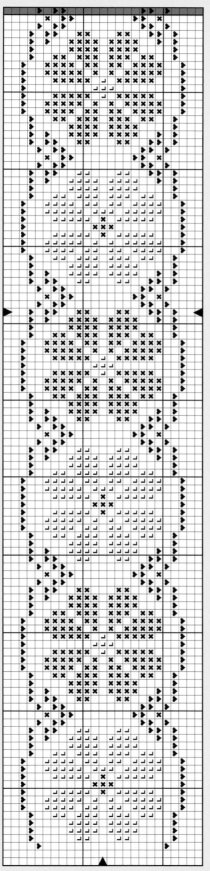

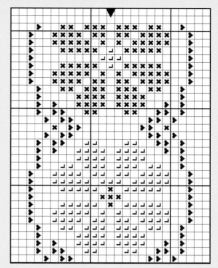

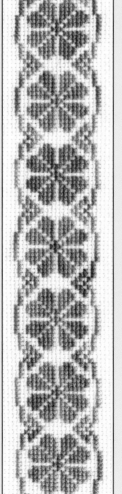

DMC Variegated	X	Str	Color
4070*	▶	3	Color variations
4126*	L	3	Color variations
4215*	✖	3	Color variations

Zinnia Zing 139w x 21h

47

KOOLER DESIGN STUDIO

Produced by:

Kooler Design Studio, Inc.
399 Taylor Blvd., Suite 104
Pleasant Hill, CA 94523
info@koolerdesign.com

Production Team:

• Creative Director: Donna Kooler
• Editor-In-Chief: Judy Swager
• Technical Editor: Priscilla Timm
• Graphic Designer: Ashley Rocha
• Photographer: Dianne Woods
• Art Director: Basha Kooler
• Technical Writer: Daline Garmon

Published by:

LEISURE ARTS
the art of everyday living

Copyright ©2010 by Leisure Arts, Inc.,
5701 Ranch Drive, Little Rock, AR 72223
www.leisurearts.com